Richard III

Published by Sweet Cherry Publishing Limited
Unit 36, Vulcan Business Complex,
Vulcan Road,
Leicester, LE5 3EF,
United Kingdom

First published in the UK in 2012
2016 edition

ISBN: 978-1-78226-238-1

©Macaw Books

Title: Richard III

Lexile® code numerical measure L = Lexile® 1130L

Text & Illustrations by Macaw Books 2012

www.sweetcherrypublishing.com

Printed and bound by Imak Ofset in Turkey

About Shakespeare

William Shakespeare, regarded as the greatest writer in the English language, was born in Stratford-upon-Avon in Warwickshire, England (around 23 April 1564). He was the third of eight children born to John and Mary Shakespeare.

Shakespeare was a poet, playwright and dramatist. He is often known as England's national poet and the 'Bard of Avon'. Thirty-eight plays, one hundred and fifty-four sonnets, two long narrative poems and several other poems are attributed to him. Shakespeare's plays have been translated into every major existent language and are performed more often than those of any other playwright.

Richard: He is the younger brother of King Edward IV and the Duke of Clarence. In the peace after the House of York has beaten Lancaster, he is jealous of his brothers and bitter about his deformed back and arm. At the start of the play he is Duke of Gloucester but through murder and manipulation he becomes King Richard III.

Queen Elizabeth: She is the wife of King Edward IV and mother of the 'Princes in the Tower' and the princess whom Richard later plans to marry. She has two sons from a previous marriage and Richard tauntingly uses her former name of 'Lady Grey'. Richard uses mistrust of her family to his advantage.

Duke of Buckingham: He is
Richard's ally until he refuses to
murder Richard's nephews, the
young princes. In return for his help,

Richard promises
to make him Earl
of Hereford but
the former queen,
Margaret, warns
Buckingham to
expect betrayal.

Queen Margaret: She is the widow of
King Henry VI who died at the end
of the civil war. She curses Elizabeth
for taking her crown and Richard for

killing her husband
and son. It is her
widowed daughter-
in-law, Lady Anne,
whom Richard
marries first.

Richard III

In the peace following years of civil war between the royal families of York and Lancaster, there lived a hunchbacked man with a withered hand and a jealous heart. His name was Richard, Duke of Gloucester.

His side, the Yorkists,
had finally won the
battle to rule England.

"Now is the winter
of our discontent made
glorious summer by this
son of York," he said.

Triumph was theirs
and all around people
celebrated – yet Richard was
not happy. He wanted to be
king himself, but instead his
older brother Edward now
sat upon the throne. Unable
to enjoy the pleasures of
peace or find a woman who
could accept his deformity,
Richard determined to
take the crown for himself.

He vowed to manipulate and murder whoever he must to get it: starting by setting his other brother, the Duke of Clarence, and the king against each other.

Richard circulated a prophecy that someone whose name began with 'G' would murder King Edward's heirs.

Soon after, the Duke of Clarence
was arrested and imprisoned in
the Tower of London. When
Richard pretended not to know
why, Clarence reminded him that
his first name was 'George' and
the king feared that *he* would be
the one to murder his children.
Richard blamed this on the king's

wife, Queen Elizabeth: "'Tis not the king that sends you to the Tower. My Lady Grey his wife, Clarence, 'tis she."

Richard also accused the queen of working with her brother to imprison Lord Hastings, who was being set free that day. The queen, he insisted, was manipulating the king. Because of her, no one was safe. Promising to help Clarence, Richard waited until he was alone to declare that he loved his brother so much he would soon send him to heaven in death.

Just then, the newly released Lord Hastings delivered the news that the king was gravely ill. Richard promised to follow Lord Hastings in visiting the king later. He resolved that he would secretly encourage him to execute Clarence so that when the king also died, Richard would be closer

to the throne. He then planned
to marry Lady Anne Neville from
the House of Lancaster, even
though he had recently killed her
husband and her father-in-law, the
former King Henry VI.

King Henry VI's
coffin was carried
through the streets

where his grieving widow Queen
Margaret and daughter-in-law,
Lady Anne, cursed the killer
and wished that his children be
deformed and his wife miserable.
Richard interrupted the funeral
procession to declare his love for
Anne, a love so strong it drove
him to kill her husband. At first

Lady Anne was disgusted, but she softened when he begged her to kill him or let him kill himself if she would not marry him. Finally, believing that he was sorry for his evil deeds, she agreed.

At the royal palace, Queen Elizabeth was worried what would happen if the king died. She

did not want Richard to become the guardian of her young son, who would inherit the throne. Two noblemen, the Duke of Buckingham and Lord Stanley, reported that the king seemed to be feeling better and wanted to meet with Richard and the queen's brothers to make peace between them. Elizabeth accused Richard of hating her and her family ever

since she switched sides after the
Lancastrians lost the war, and
Richard accused Elizabeth of
orchestrating the imprisonment of
both Clarence and Lord Hastings.

The former queen, Margaret,
entered unnoticed as they argued.
She blamed Elizabeth for the theft
of her crown and Richard for the

death of her husband and son.
Meanwhile Earl Rivers, Queen
Elizabeth's brother, who benefitted
greatly from her marriage, insisted
that they were not traitors but loyal
followers of whoever was king.

"Hear me, you wrangling
pirates," said the old queen,
Margaret, who thought they

were all as bad as each other.
To Richard she claimed, "A
husband and a son thou ow'st
to me"; to Queen Elizabeth,
"And thou a kingdom." She
cursed Elizabeth to live to
see her own children die and
another woman take her throne.
She hoped Elizabeth's brother,
Lord Rivers, and her son from
a previous marriage, Lord
Grey, would die too. Queen
Margaret cursed them and
Lord Hastings for standing
by as her son was murdered.
Richard she condemned to
be plagued with suspicions
and to believe his friends were
traitors while taking traitors

as his closest friends. Lastly
she warned Buckingham that
Richard would betray him.

A nobleman called Catesby
who served Richard brought the
news that the king wished to see
them all. Richard was pleased that
he had managed to convince so

many that Queen Elizabeth was to blame for Clarence's imprisonment. He sent two murderers to kill Clarence immediately. Meanwhile the sickly King Edward IV greeted his visitors and urged them to be friends. They all agreed, but when Queen Elizabeth asked the king to

accept Clarence back into his good graces, Richard revealed that he was already dead. Everyone was shocked, especially King Edward, who had sent a message to pardon Clarence. His health became worse and he soon died.

Buckingham agreed with Richard that they should protect the young prince and future king from the bad influence of his

mother and her followers. Soon
after, the queen learned that
Earl Rivers, Lord Grey, and her

friend Sir Thomas Vaughan had been imprisoned. She thought she and her children would be targeted next. The Cardinal granted sanctuary to Queen Elizabeth but Buckingham insisted that her other royal son, the young prince's brother, should attend the coronation.

Until then, Richard suggested that both children stay in the Tower for their safety.

Since the prince was too young to rule, Richard had become Lord Protector of England, but he wanted more. Richard, Buckingham and Catesby plotted to make Richard king instead. However, Catesby was concerned that Lord Hastings would not support them, even though he and Richard were friends. Hastings hated the queen's family, but had loved the late King Edward IV. Furthermore, Lord Stanley would do whatever

Hastings did. If Hastings
did not cooperate, Richard
declared, "Chop off his head!"

Richard planned to
execute the queen's captive
followers the next day and even
though he was not yet king, he

promised to give Buckingham
the earldom of Hereford for all
his help. Catesby had been sent
to convince Lord Hastings to
support Richard's claim to the
throne. Hastings was happy to
learn that the queen's family were
to be killed but could not support

his friend Richard taking the crown from the young prince.

Earl Rivers, Lord Grey, and Sir Thomas Vaughn were executed. Before he died, Rivers prayed that Richard, Hastings and Buckingham would soon meet their share of Queen Margaret's

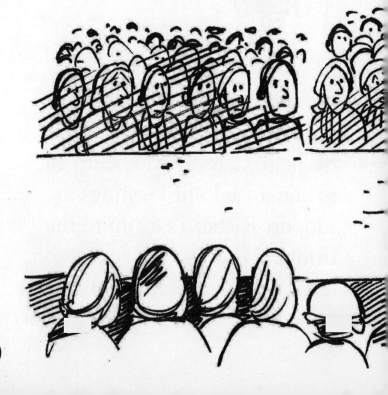

curse, but that Queen Elizabeth and her children would be spared.

At a council meeting to discuss the coronation of the young king, the assembly decided to crown him the next day. Richard and Buckingham talked privately of Hastings refusing to join their scheme,

while Hastings continued to believe that Richard was good and true.

When Richard returned from his talk he was furious, claiming to have learnt that his deformed arm was a result of witchcraft cast against him by Queen Elizabeth. He accused Hastings of conspiring

with her and ordered his execution: "Off with his head!"

Hastings' head was brought before the Lord Mayor. Richard and Buckingham pretended to be sad over the treachery, and the mayor was convinced that Hastings must have deserved execution

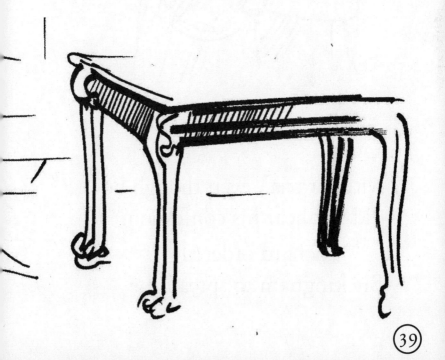

without trial, even though he
did not hear his confession.

Richard ordered
Buckingham to spread the

rumour that King Edward's sons
were illegitimate and not rightful
heirs to the throne. The citizens
were not convinced and didn't
seem to want Richard to become
king. To mend his bad reputation,
Richard pretended that he would
not take the crown if the public
did not want him to. Buckingham
made a speech saying it would be
treason for Richard not to save

England from the rule of an illegitimate heir. Still Richard pretended to feel reluctant and unworthy. Finally Buckingham declared that this was because Richard loved his nephew too much to depose him, but that he must – for the good of the people. Finally, Richard agreed and was hailed Richard III, King of England.

Queen Elizabeth and her companions were prevented from visiting the princes in the Tower and learnt that Richard

was now king and soon to be
married to Lady Anne Neville.
Like Elizabeth, Anne believed
that she was the victim of a
curse: her own. In wishing that
Richard's wife would be unhappy,
she had damned herself as she
had no choice but to marry him.
She worried that Richard would
soon kill her. Lord Stanley, who
brought the news, was worried
that his stepson, the Earl of

Richmond, could be in danger
since he was also in line for the
throne. He promised to send word
to warn him and to ask him to
give protection to anyone escaping
England and its new king.

True to the old queen
Margaret's curse, Richard

was a paranoid king. When
Buckingham could not bring
himself to murder the two
princes, Richard replaced him
with Sir James Tyrell. Richard
had learnt that the Marquess
of Dorset, the former queen
Elizabeth's other son, had fled

to join Richmond. With the
princes dead, Richard planned to
marry their sister to strengthen
his kingship, but first he ordered
Catesby to spread a rumour that
Queen Anne was deathly ill.

Richard ignored
Buckingham's reminder that

he was supposed to be given
the earldom of Hereford for his
loyal service and Buckingham
decided to flee to Wales before
he ended up like Hastings.
Already predicting a civil war
with Richmond, especially
since King Henry VI had

once predicted that Richmond
would become king, Richard
warned Lord Stanley not to let
his wife, Richmond's mother,
send any letters to her son.

Tyrell returned and reported
that the princes were dead.
He had hired two other men
to do it since even he could

not bring himself to smother
children. Richard was delighted
and promised to reward Tyrell
handsomely. Meanwhile Queen
Anne had died and Richard
had imprisoned Clarence's son
and married off his daughter so
that neither would be threats
to his crown. Richmond was

gaining support so Richard set out to start wooing his niece knowing that Richmond wanted to marry her himself. He even asked Queen Elizabeth to speak to her daughter on his behalf.

More and more people abandoned Richard's side to join Richmond's. When Lord Stanley brought a report that

Richmond had arrived to seize
the throne, Richard accused him
of helping the enemy – why else
had he not brought troops with
him? Richard sent him to gather
his men but demanded that he
leave his son behind as insurance

that those men would fight *for* Richard and not against him.

Lord Stanley held a secret meeting with a priest on Richmond's side. He could not fight with them openly without endangering his son, but he sent word from Queen Elizabeth

that she would be happy for
Richmond to marry her daughter.

Richmond's army made
camp near Richard's at Bosworth
Field in Leicester. Richard was
pleased that Richmond had
far fewer troops than he did,
but Richmond's men had been
strengthened by speeches of hope

and peace, while Richard's men were unhappy and fearful. Among Richard's men was Lord Stanley, who had been passing information to his stepson. Richard had instructed Lord Stanley to bring his troops before sunrise, "lest his son George fall into the blind cave of eternal night". So

Lord Stanley went secretly to Richmond's camp and told him to be prepared for battle early next morning. He promised to mislead Richard's troops in whatever way he could, while still appearing to be loyal for the safety of his captive son.

That night Richard, who drank wine and slept early, was visited by the ghosts of all those he had killed, who condemned him to "Despair and die!" To Richmond, who had made his preparations

long into the night, the same ghosts bade him to "Awake, and win the day." Richard knew that he was a villain and refused to

pity himself, but the dream had
frightened him as it foretold
that this would be his final
battle. Meanwhile Richmond's
dream had encouraged him
and he led his troops into
battle with a rousing speech.

Richard's speech was far less
inspiring and interrupted by news

that Lord Stanley would not
be bringing his troops after all.
There was no time for Richard
to kill Stanley's son before the
battle, so he vowed to do it after
– but he never got the chance.

On the battlefield Richard
hunted for Richmond on
foot crying "A horse, a horse,

my kingdom for a horse!" Finally, after killing several decoys, Richard found the real Richmond. The two fought fiercely and Richard was slain. Lord Stanley plucked the crown from his body and Richmond was crowned King Henry VII. All the soldiers who had fought so unwillingly on the tyrant Richard's side were forgiven and England was unified. With the marriage of the new king from

the Lancastrian line to the
daughter of Queen Elizabeth
and the late King Edward
IV of the line of York the
War of the Roses was finally
over after thirty-two years.